INTRODUCTION

The tradition continues.

In this sixth volume of the series, three more new voices in South Australian poetry give fresh insights into subjects as diverse as fishing, mid-life crises and of course, love – anxious, sweet, bitter or nostalgic.

Buy it. Get three fresh handles on life. You won't regret it.

David Cookson
CONVENOR,
FRIENDLY STREET POETS

FRIENDLY STREET

new poets six

Rain Falls on the Garden, John De Laine
Fish Star Glinting, Alison Manthorpe
maiden voyage, Ray R. Tyndale

Friendly Street Poets

WAKEFIELD
PRESS

Friendly Street Poets Incorporated
in association with
Wakefield Press
17 Rundle Street
Kent Town
South Australia 5071

First Published 2000

Cover illustration by Jonathon Inverarity
Book design and typesetting by Tabloid Pty Ltd, Adelaide
Printed and bound by Hyde Park Press, Adelaide

ISBN 1 86254 509 X

Friendly Street is supported by the South Australian
Government through Arts SA.

ARTSA

CONTENTS

RAIN FALLS ON THE GARDEN
by John De Laine

John De Laine was born in Adelaide, South Australia, in 1969.
He studies the professional writing course at Adelaide TAFE,
and has worked before in the textile industry and as a temporary
public servant. He's single and lives in Adelaide.

ACKNOWLEDGEMENTS

Friendly Street Readers 22/23 for 'Shade' and 'Cleaning Rome', originally titled 'A Roman Girl Washes'; *Southerly* for 'Reputation'; *Hobo* for 'After Five'; *Social Alternatives* for 'Network'; *Core* for 'Who Speaks for the Lemon Tree?', which was originally titled 'Lemon Tree Rights in Pre-Wik Australia'; *Home Brew* for 'It's a Girl'; *Centoria* for 'Lover and Wife'; *The Gawler Bunyip* for 'Plaza'; *Gathering Force* for 'Good Grooming'; *Imagination* for 'Love Birds', 'Choose the Future', 'Italian Girl' and 'Seeds', which was originally titled 'Growing'.

Sincere thanks to the editors; the above poems appear in this collection as largely revised versions.

I dedicate this collection to Melva De Laine
my mother
and my greatest supporter

THE POEMS

Mirage

Hands sift a channel cut into
a sandgrain sea
adrift on a hot noon

miles west
of the great snake
River Nile

Hands on the upslope
of a dune
that swallows knees

Hands crawl
against the tick tock
of forever lost

In sight of a dream
oasis which stings eyes
with salvation and women

of honey blood
Lazing nude
in poses olive oil

and hands
are waved to help them

But fertile mindplains
run deep
within headache

skulls
Bring only the pictures
of greener grass

It's a Girl

His perspective

She waits in the corner
of his eye
Stands on the sad edge
of his life
getting wet from the tears
within shadows he crys
over her
He tells friends
there must be a used-by date
on her wedding finger
In the forest
where couples live smug
her heart's lost among trees

Her perspective

His heart muscles are lazy
She hates him
for that
She knows he knows
in the bones
that her soul is fresh bread
He's drank spirit
and work
Why can't he drink
deep from life's third cup?
The honesty inside
shouts at him
that she's someone special

The Defectors

A woman and a man hold two of the furthest outposts
both of them fatigued   Hardened border guards in a war
no one will admit is wrong

Between them lies
the high fence of misunderstanding   Built of cold steel wire
it is a monument to the material years

After the Sunday rain and snow   the hurt of nothing more
than tokenist equality   these guards feel again a wind
of change that slaloms through timbertown tall

and so they move closer   to the fence   Face to face

Now the man wraps a finger round rusted razor
barbs   there to protect the '90s from nature
She watches tears trek beneath his eyes   They drop

machine guns in the snow as birds
watch through the forest   Mittens off   She claws at the wire
with hands that cut and bleed and wish to cradle a baby

Moves a finger through   against the blades and rust
to find a home along his thumb
Sees her future in the shy smile he offers as surrender

Love Birds

Traffic drones its endless hum
that travels past the birds
as they try to share a private moment
Some quality family time
in the nest   Beaks buried
in feathered chests
devoted chirps for all the right tunes
A bit of post-dinner affection
and after-worm get-together
is on their minds
Preening feathers to get libido up
they peek out over the lip
of woven twigs and nature's twine
Spy on the melee of humanity below
Wish for some fucking
privacy   Sweet symphonies
of running water or the paisley mellow
of an early Pink Floyd track
LP for ages after the long hard day
      Them's cool waves
for copulation   Lots of Gen-X babies
were conceived to that sound
which echoed beyond the rich walls
of mothers' wombs
Kept safe within democracy bedrooms
far from the screams
and frantic flash of bloody Vietnam
The birds we know today
have only the shell of a golden egg

Must go wild high up
in dying branches laced with smog
Find spots and orgasms
among blaring horns   exhausts
backfired   Jackhammers   Tenderless

Who Speaks for the Lemon Tree?

As ideas are still the lightbulbs
above a smart head
Before workmen crowd round
plans in hand
  to give sky pie quotes
the lemon tree's alone

Hemmed in between the rusted iron
of suburban corrugation
and changes

Unable to hold on
the tree's fruit goes to ground
Is collected
from ungrassed earth that hoops
a crooked trunk
Is squeezed

for its bitter blood
Is thrown
hard into the heart
of an Aussie-made wastebin
Is not told
about the summer's day

when its juice stings
cold in the workmen's mouths
As they tear the tree from its place
As it dies
for a swimming pool
in the tray of a noisy truck

After Five

The bad social butterfly
The one with grime
on its awkward wings
smog mingles and schmoozes
with the big noise

Flirts with noses
is bought drinks by the rain

Never misses a chance
to gatecrash
streetside gatherings
of the Mondayitis Club
People weary

from the l o n g day
Looking for taxis

    buses
    love

Who go nose up
at the jagged shudder

of exhausts not Ultra-tuned
Who watch the faces
in the cars
curse
    sigh

    try to remember
how to get to St Tropez

Made to Fit

Sandals were never in trend
at high school
Those were the days
when my embryonic poetry
was pulped underfoot
by the boot of better careers

and sandals told the story
of a boy told what to do
for years

Sandals were imprisoned
in the real world
of a dark wardrobe dungeon
the whims of fashion
against them
They did some hard time

but they were strong
Those sandals were made
for growing in

and when I found them
    years later
and freed them from that place
their little buckles jingled
Jingled to the distant music
of a child running

hard into his life ahead

The Human Movie

comes in over-budget   too short
the edges scratched
the whole production hyper-hyped
to blur the grey of critics
Actors roll and tumble
in studio stardust
wanting so much to be like
Keystone Cops

and wanting
so much to be liked

There are no out-takes
Few second
chances
Too many lines are left
unspoken
Most intercourse
is filmed in black and white
and each law made's

another stage prop moved
into someone's
shrinking space
The script we're asked
to follow
has no author
and every day screens
more of the reruns

Same reruns same reruns same

Declare War

on loneliness
– Hold someone's hand today!

Steel

In shadows of a skyscraper
flesh feels
the earthquake of change
restless in attitude

On a dark uprising that plots
against the meek

These years have made it hard
as reinforced steel
the womb's feather walls
road dust

I can see
a steel compactus
pressing in and in
Movement

against the shape of dreams

I see lives trapped under
the hammer
Knives out and getting sharper
Necks more sore

from constant turning
to look behind
Sleep fractured by the sound
of rustling paper...

Triplicate forms
and the headache of bills unpaid
Love letters of the ages
blown up against

cyclone fences and forgotten

Plaza

The terrace flagstones cool
from daytime's throb
of blister
Dark sneaks into place
before a fading sky
to ambush cacti soldiers
splash shadows
across distant huddles
of pretty sedum flowers
Foreground
for a mesa stage
Dark slides
across empty desert spaces
to find the stony edge
of plaza floor
Where human noise
and the fall

of women's hair
collides with the brilliance
of a Mexican dusk
They are the people
of pain
They remain
to paint a sky of baby night
an explosive rainbow
of hissing   rocket   colour
Remain to flirt
hands on skirt and shirt

Hear cries from devils
horny in a sensuous trance
Who dance on tables
swim in serenades
from unshaven musicians
in big black sombreros

Good Grooming

From her navel is plucked
an ancient pinch of lint...
    Good work
Ninety-nine   Max would say

See the splashes of hair
night-black strands
of spider silk
Spilling down in twisty locks
brushed in gushes
    and the body...
that x-tra Revlon shine
blinds the eyes
Each dark and touched up
seductive scanners
of feline perfection
Ready for the wild of night

    and see the neat red work
of art   her painted lips
as she releases in a husky whisper
onto mirror glass

– her score
  out of ten

A New Leaf

Merry-go-round past
ends for a man
with dirt in his soul
Dark pleasure
has reached its limit
of suffering

but the autumn
will heal
with its tide of leaves
He can forget
weakness
and he can remember

forever
If he tries hard
empty lust
will age
into an old witch
before winter comes

Cleaning Rome

Soon after the sundial passes
to mark noon
she nears the water's edge
arms outstretched and yawning
For forgiveness
For last night

She kneels beside the pool
and cups
life in hungry hands
Splashes sleep
and dead dreams
from staleface woman

The water returns a spark
to eyes heavy
from too much shallow
flatter flutter
It leaves random drops
on long locks

of hair scribbled in hot curls
Moonless across
hammerbash forehead
over eartops
and down both sides
of schoolgirl grin

She rises to shed silk
The clothing
lost in scents of red wine
and don't care cocksuck
Melts nude body into water
to forget about sin

Italian Girl

Her eyes are dark and deep
wide with passion
and glisten hungrily
for the feast of love
Breasts await a tender touch

and lips mime kisses that say
    She Will Love
Her hair silk black which shines
below a noon sun
Gentle hands caress and cradle

its locks
    She Will Dream
Her soft skin sweats slow
in warm air
Dark as old honey

it keeps her soul inside
from exploding out
She counts days for days
sips her red wine
washes herself in deep

electric blue
    She Will Always Be
a princess
of the Adriatic
a flame of much desire

Gentle Power

Today she's bathed in a giant
clam of warm milk
Nudity is nothing to her
as she rises
allowing a warm spring breeze
to dry her sculpture
Soak up all the droplets
from coal hair

She has moved on down
her power halls
spending smiles on her servants
Warm in the sunshine
that walks in through windows
slit against arrows
in the overcast of some old battle
Listening
to the diamond advice
of birds in trees beyond

She has settled soft against
the purple velvet
of her throne
Declared that peace
shall pound in every heart
Babies kick
within excited mothers' wombs
and a Million Years' War
will be waged against
the hollow ruin of loneliness

Blind Foreplay

His offer of balls ripe
and in a bunch

fat with seeds in maturity
packed stiff

and swollen
with sweetness that oozes

Each one randomly selected
by tongue swerve

Smashed
by white razors

and swallowed slow
and down a slender ride

of lovebitten throat
ignites her

to part flame lips
for more   and   more

Until a stocking silk
of blindfold

is removed
and the roles reversed

Lover and Wife

He likes his wife
for her audible commentary on dreams
she can never remember
The way she snores like a mouse
rolls over in bed
into his arms without waking
Stays there till light
The way sunflakes knock at the lids
of his closed eyes

    creeping in before
the clock radio explodes into a morning
madness that rips serenity
to shreds
– he snooze-buttons it

as she murmurs stale-breath nothings
    sniffs
    sighs
    rubs
her feet against each other

with rebel friction beneath
blankets and sheets
Fighting dawn's oppressive chill
He likes to be holding
her hand when she wakes
takes in

her first impressions of the day
Utters early words
through sensuous lips revealing
the smile of a woman
who sleeps

with her husband
and wakes with her lover

Seeds

Nature is on the telly
of a kitchen window
She cuts out the ads
from inside

Holding it together
          its stars
are seeds on their own
in suburban ground

in constant call
for help from the sky
answered always
by the fade of the blue

The dark battleship
of rainclouds full and sad
She sees them
feels it kick

recalls the sun's voice
in her ear
one Sunday afternoon
in the long meadow grass

She watches
as rain falls on the garden
and wishes for nothing
but sunshine

on a baby seed
that grows from her sex

Choose the Future

You pick at your brains
about getting it right
once
and for all

You know to divide brain
from heart from
a cholesterol bank balance
a burning desire

to miss the road fork
But you fail
Must make a choice
don't stall

don't ever think
too hard
Stick a nervous neck
out too far

You bite bullets
prepare to ride your wave

Cast doubt
from the highest cliff

and die when it's time to
Without wondering

The School

Little spurts of silver dart
as winks drowning
beneath a whitecapped roof
of cresting waves
that mark the stormfront

A whole generation
still learning

Behind breakwater they flow
as a family
embracing the danger
Until one is lured
to a wriggling tempt of death

and blubs swearmarine
through lips
of nature's delicate rubber
Slit by hook and leaving
blood behind

Moving on
the school glides through
a shipwreck
Does loops between
the decks that once were

Network

Screen pings on my mind
Changes gear
from the lush and timeless words
of favourite nightcap poets
to bits binary
byting at my fertile thoughts

My actions cleansed
by a viral scan
the cyberworld beckons me
like a Kings Cross pimp
Pleads for me
to shrink the planet

Watch boundaries fade away
like dying TV tubes
See laws of tax and trade
gather dust on bookshelves
along decision corridors
I'm a spider

spinning work at my Net
lost for hours on a surf safari
Take in glimpses of scenes
and samples and places and faces
What remains
of all human traces

I'm nothing like my friends
They sit stunned
through a lifetime of subliminal ads
not happy with this channel
or liking that one
Eyes square on their world

Shade

It's Sunday and the sun
is on its way
down

I look up to find
cool darkness
all above
and feel the grass
at my back
Hear water warble
in a stream
that runs by my feet
Calming
like a woman's touch
the throb of ego
in my chest
Green drifts down
to me from patches
of botanic moss
The words
of my favourite poets
still giggle
in my ears
I hear a honey lute
gently plucked
by a bearded minstrel
who catches sunrays
in the nearby
olive grove

While the shade
of my tree
protects me like a parent

Peacekeepers

Rain may never stop
The tanks

roll over more teddies
in mud beds

Face down
and no more hugs

Shellshock
   guncry soldiers

   shout of more blood
More

Old people shuffling
into chaos

Shoeless children in tears
their mothers

with legs open
to keep the peace today

Stalemate at Ypres

Gas masks are the animal face
of tired virgins
who remember sky
as blue
Grass and the young leaves
wearing green

Here the mud is the curse
of free men
Barbed wire the prison of those same
free men
Shrapnel an end
to eyefuls of pretty girls

Death the reward
for love of country and king

Wage slavers
and snugglebed sovereigns
… all sing

Reputation

The writer gets drunk
on the wine
of free expression
whenever he speaks
– slurs to groups
of discerning people
in the know
Who wear clothes in vogue
and nod at things
they don't understand

He lets his silver fly
fly low
and expose the hidden hardness
of each syllable
In every word he spills
lets dribble down
his stubbled chin
to splash on Hoovered carpet
Leaving stains and making
permanent remarks

FISH STAR GLINTING
by **Alison Manthorpe**

Alison Manthorpe grew up on a farm, worked as a physiotherapist,
married a master mariner and accompanied him to sea in yachts.
She is now retired to Coffin Bay with time to write.

ACKNOWLEDGEMENTS

The Bunyip for the first poem of the 'Farmyard' sequence.
Hobo for 'The dark sea' and 'Edge'.

Special thanks to mentor Jan Owen and members of Eyre
Writers, and also to SA Writers' Centre and Country Arts SA for
their support of country writers over the years, particularly their
support for this country writer.

For D.P.M.

THE POEMS

The Dark Sea

He is gone from me
to where horizons
flat as a knife blade
cut the seaman loose
from earth's substantial logic.

Only seabirds balanced on air
watch where he works
sleeps
lives out his days
balanced on water,
ploughing the heaving swells
of ocean.

Swinging
poised between ocean and sky,
he is balanced too finely
for my peace,
over the tumbling chasms
of the ever-changing,
never-changing
dark sea I celebrate
and fear.

Implacable, uncaring,
the ocean
shares my love's love with me.

Edge

Where sea meets earth
on long beaches
sandpipers bob,
scuttle on invisible feet down the pale benches
nimble as blown thistledown.
Smooth ranks of sea rush in,
smash to lace fringes against the sand,
let loose a wash of lullaby sound
that crowds the salt-sticky air.
Empty cowries, rolled in by the surf,
trap earfuls of it.
Like blood, the song fades and surges,
stirs echoes in restless boys
with earth-dust on their boots.

Viking Departure

Above the estuary the reeds whip and bend,
raked by a cold spring wind
that carries the bleating, the reek of damp wool,
and the scream of seagulls wheeling and dipping;
that tugs at beards newly trimmed to clear the oars,
that carries the shouts and the laughter.

At the sea's fringe
beyond the trampled sands and the scattered bundles
the fierce prows rear in line like angry swans.

The men muster,
put their shoulders to the ships' shoulders,
heave, curse at the catch of a keel on pebbles,
grunt out crude promises –
this year they'll take more gold, more girls, more plunder
than other marauding crews.
Shoving, swearing, worn boots digging,
they run the ships down the beach
into the slipping waves,
scramble, wet legs kicking, over the gunnels
and feel beneath their feet the first seas lifting.

And when the bleating is silenced
and hot sheep's blood runs down the planking,
Orm Sveinsson remembers
a man's blood can spurt as easily,
as casually,
and he prays the sea gods
will drink their fill
from the sheep.

Homecoming

When the sun burst up
we were sweating already,
heaving oars through a sea clogged with weariness.
The wind had left us on the second day.

Naxos
had dropped below the sea-line,
Ariadne, that sad princess,
gone with it.
Abandoned, with no explanations.
And none of us knew what she'd done
that had so enraged Theseus.
He was in a foul mood still
three days after he'd left her,
brooding alone in the stern
staring over the wake,
gazing south.
Perhaps he was wishing her back.
That's the trouble with these lusty heroes,
reflexes splendid for battle but
too quick by half for peace.
Only Amyntor
was brave enough to go near him.

So when the breeze got up and we hoisted the sail,
the black canvas bellying overhead filled
with a soft sweet breeze that set the sea dancing,
and all of us thankful to run the oars inboard,
Theseus didn't notice for a while.
Poseidon's temple, small on Sounion,
had fallen astern before he looked round.

We saw his face. But
no matter how loudly he shouted, cursed us and swore,
while we broke our fingernails clawing at halliards,
yanking at sheets cleated hard,
we could not get the damned sail down
before half Athens saw it,
and shouted the news to his father, where he paced
on the high rim of the Acropolis.

So it was into his own kingdom
Theseus stepped
and welcomed us home.

Song for an Ocean Voyager

He has put out from shore,
sailed through seas green as a mermaid's eye
to where dark ocean,
the deep and dark blue ocean, rolls
to meet the sky.

Where the long swells heave up astern
to dwarf the helmsman,
an albatross hangs aloft scanning the wake,
and whales, long spines awash like upturned hulls,
spurt vapour fountains
and curve their bodies under.

Where waves like giant hands slap the hull,
spray hits like gravel,
salt stings his lips,
and the cold air he drinks
is clean and sharp as thin dry wine.

Where in the shouting gales
the ocean smokes water ripped
from the crests by a shrieking wind
that falls like a wall on the trysail
and drives the rail under.

Where in days of blue sunshine
the drowsy plain slides with gold,
a sea-snake, curled asleep,
rocks in a hammock of water,
and volleys of flying fish
burst through the sea's skin
like arrows
on stiff wings.

Where he follows
over heaving unmarked ocean
tracks of older seamen
who sailed uncharted seas,
hazarding their lives, their ships,
to complete the maps.

And in the night
those dumpy wooden hulls,
lifting and swinging across the seas,
scribbled their pencil masts against the heavens,
traced the same patterns
the new voyager sees his masthead tracing
against the same white stars.
The moon swims fathoms deep under his keel.

Louisiade Archipelago, July 1606

Late on a soft grey afternoon two ships
sailed into Oba Bay. High on the forested hills
surrounding them, banners of misty rain
drifted across the green canopies.
And once the anchors were down
silence returned like a presence
except for the plops of rain from the rigging
and a bird hooting from the sodden leaves.
Torres called the bay Puerto de San Francisco.

They'd been five days along the coral,
standing off at night, sail shortened, watches doubled,
in daylight making north of west, believing
peaks of distant islands to be one land.
When the reef sank safely they'd come north
searching for a way to Manila.

Natives watched from the beaches
but when the boats went in
fled to the hills. The Spaniards followed
up dark tracks between the trees
and found the gardens, where they dug yams
from earth like black putty.
A transient gleam of sunlight lit them,
new actors on an old stage.

For fifteen days the boats explored the islands
Sideia and Sariba, Doini,
giving them saintly Spanish titles,
taking vegetables and pigs, shooting a cuscus
and some of the natives who opposed them
in war canoes.

In a wet dawn the boats were hauled aboard,
the capstans creaked the anchors up, the yards blossomed sail,
and the two ships stood out across the bay,
sailing westward for the mainland
and the undiscovered strait.

West MacDonnell Ranges

Dry gully

Ribbons of bark
rustle like snakeskins underfoot.
Mallees curtsey in the wind
and fill the gully with singing.
In the leaf litter
a rust red skink, striped black,
hides in stillness;
its nerve fails; it flicks away
under the stones.
Gone
like a word on the tip of my tongue.

Ochre

I would like
to flit through the dreaming ranges
knowing the lore and the secrets,
reading the signs,
living the stories told by the rocks.
I would go barefoot,
naked and stippled with ochre
and have no fear of splinters
or sunburn.

This is my land. But my stories
come from a different hemisphere,
and are told by different rocks –
by rings of standing stones,
menhirs, rune stones, cromlechs.

Rockface

I offer thanks to the old heroic gods
who stacked those blocks,
painted those colours,
built that sheer red wall,
that I have strength to walk here,
eyes to see,
space in my memory
before age tethers me,
darkens my sight
and knots my bones.

Above, a white stemmed eucalypt
small from high distance,
spills a brace of jade green parrots.

Listening for the Tooth Fairy

Lying between cold sides-to-middled sheets,
the night dews flowing in through the flywire
to chill my skin,
the moon sticky-beaking under the eaves
like a rude staring eye backing towards the west,
and the cooling iron roof cracking
like gunshots at the barking foxes,
I heard from miles away the distant thunder
of steel rails grinding under steely wheels
driven by beats of steam. Though knowing this –
that rails defined the monster's headlong rush –
I trembled that the beast would charge the flats
and in my iron beadstead flatten me.

Eleanor

In a heatwave my sister
took pity on her little cat
and set out to sponge it cool.
It detested the water but
was held by her voice. Tensely,
ears flattened, it crouched
while she soaked it to the skin.

She knew animals
with a respect beyond sentiment
and wept for the snake she killed
for safety at the back door

We were two halves
of one imagination and her quirks
were leaven to mine.

Frost laid thin ice
on the puddle outside the garage.
She'd lift the crackling glass sheets
while her hands turned purple with cold
and I laughed unkindly at the colour.
We crunched ice in our teeth
mud and all.

Her fingers have outgrown chilblains
and draw up shapely bowls
pots, platters, jugs,
from clots of muddy clay.
Long highways intervene
between her imagination and mine.

Farmyard 1930s

The cowshed was brush,
melalueca uncinata, cut
from scrub close to the house.
The thatch started out weather proof
but with age grew bald.
So Dad pitch-forked straw up
to keep out the rain.
The roof grew a fine crop of oats
that spring.
The fenced yard around it
never grew grasses or weeds.
Too many hoofs crossing
kept it trampled to deep sand,
a Sahara heaven
for chooks to fluff through their feathers
and hot sweating horses to roll in.

❏

Four geese
which my father bought from a mate
at an RSL meeting
when he wasn't concentrating
turned out to be peacocks.
A cock and three hens.
The male was very beautiful
showing off his gaudy tail,
but he ate all the new ducklings.

A fox ate the hens.

❏

The pet lamb Saint George
lived estranged from his kind.
He left the back door when he grew older
and joined the cows.
Morning and evening
he followed them in to the milking
and followed them out to graze.
In his heart
George knew he was a cow.

❏

When the farm was new
and my mother hung clothes to dance in the wind
a mob of curious emus
stalked out of the uncleared scrub
across the Plover Paddock
to the cowyard fence
and paced about peering and craning.

Two nesting magpies streaked down like Stukas
and attacked the emus' periscope heads.

The emus ducked
from the snapping beaks,
dodging and
dancing as though
they would lift their long legs
and swat
the damned birds.

❏

The three sheepdogs,
black with white collars
and tan eyebrows expressive as their buoyant tails,
lived half their time chained
under the pines.
Budge was named
for a male American tennis star
but was female, and liberated.
At shearing Mum had to chain her up
for half an hour at mornings and middays
or intent on her job
she followed the men to the wool-shed
and neglected to feed her pups.

❏

The shearer said my bay horse Toby
was hard as nails
and game as Ned Kelly.
I knew this for truth
but hadn't his command of language
to express it myself.

❏

When Dad electrified part of a fence
the pigs were too confused
to disengage.
They froze to the wire
and squealed like ungreased axles.

But my sister's black horse Rocket,
a spoilt pet sharp as a tack,
learned to listen at the box
for the make and break clicking,
and only in silence did he
lean on the hay-yard fence
to steal hay.

Outdoor Dining Table

Over next door's fence
the sun rises, and ignites green fires
in the empty wine bottle.
Fossicker ants search for pay dirt
round the dead hurricane lantern
and scurry off to bank their treasure.
The blue biro has rolled across
a chain of wine-stained rings
to a racing program
from Largs Bay Sailing Club.

Glossy yellow, a half lemon
squeezed to the last drop
like the argument over censorship
is a reminder of the snapper
baked in foil.

By the black-handled knife
a leather watch band curls up
like pleading fingers.
A mug pink as lawyers' tape
weights a torn page scribbled with
dollar sums, thumbnail horses,
and three lines of a limerick
going nowhere.

A boxed de Bortoli shiraz cabernet
presides four-square at the table's head.
Slowly
the shadow of the trellis spreads a grid
across the dark boards of the table.

Mario

So I move north
to Port Pirie, Port Augusta.
Looked like it might be a good place
this new country
but not working for my uncle
or those lying bastards my cousins.
So I left Virginia.
Nineteen twenty-five and jobs hard to find.

Fortunes, says the bearded bloke
in the front bar of the Northern,
make a fortune gouging opal.
You know, Andamooka. I buy him a pint
and I've still enough left for a bike.

The sun burns a hole in the sky
big as Calabria,
sucks the land dry, withers my throat, pedalling
always pedalling towards lakes of mirage
over a damn road like the goat tracks
up the mountains behind Reggio,
just as stony, only flat.
Flat on the crumbling bones of this dead country.

Forty years and there's no pot of gold,
but I like it here. Suits me.
So I scratch a living searching for chips of the rainbow.
Cheap. I'm not bothered with rent.
I dug a hole through the bones,
a place to live
underground. Like the opal.

Mrs P and Mrs S

The junior nurse
ties Mrs Parker's sparse white hair
in a pink ribbon.
A Lancashire lass over seventy years ago,
Mrs Parker is not impressed.
'As a nurse,' she says,
'she's not a bad hairdresser.'

Mrs Stratford, a hundred not out,
and born in Yorkshire,
laughs heartily and tells her frail daughter,
inmate of a different nursing home,
'You'll have to finish me off with an axe, dear.'
Young nurses who tease their Strattie
are soon put right.
'Don't,' she says, peering from her used-up eyes,
'call me a whingeing Pom, miss.
I've lived in this country
longer than you have.'

In the Physio room
where Mrs Parker meets Mrs Stratford,
staff are entertained by a brisk exchange
in the ongoing Wars of the Roses.
The old women cackle evilly and remember
the rude chants each recited
against the other county
in schoolyards and in pubs:
Lancastrian and Yorkist
refusing to lay down their arms.

The Wooden Knife

This wooden paper-knife
my father carved
from a piece of mulga wood he picked up
near Uluru
before the roads were made
and the first campers bumped in –
so long ago he needed a permit
to follow the faint tracks.

In the farm workshop, walled with chicken wire
to stop chooks roosting on his tools,
he locked the dark hardwood
in the vice and planed it flat,
then with a tenon-saw cut the shape
long and tapering,
carved out the blade with his pocket knife,

pared it thin,
and sanded the wood
smooth as worn silver.

The myriad things my mother made
we ate, or wore to rags.

The Lantern

In the shed, the dark
the lantern grounded
burning a hole in the darkness
lighting his boots, the unshod hoofs.
The smell of manure in the straw
the hoofs stamping
a rippling snort of the nostrils
the mane shaking. The bit jingles.
He curses.

She says, 'You'll be back.'

He yanks up the girth through the buckles.
'Who knows?'

Both hear the thud of guns
on distant battlefields.
She flinches, her hand
on his arm.

The dog crouching, light on its watchful eyes
the head lifting. A shadow
leaps up the iron walls.

The reek of hot kerosene
the hurricane lantern flaring. Black smoke
clouds the side of the round glass.
A cold wind stirs the straw.

His Hands She Remembers

workman's hands
black grease of engines a barked knuckle
the scar where the chisel slipped

with this ring the scent of lilies
squeezing her fingers
brushing the veil her cheek

chucking the kids up catching
jellybones breath safe
and sound laughter

tomorrow
is tomorrow and tomorrow
creeping too soon poor shadow

his hands holding
shoulders the lost bird the
steering wheel cocooned in headlights
reflections the night
lightly on her skin stroking
away fears for
his hands she remembers
his hands
patting the dog
gripping her fingers
letting go.

Budgerigars

They rise up in a cloud
flying fast, a shadowed swirl
against the flat blue inland sky.
The swarm extends, contracts, and wheels,
a twisting genie shape dancing
over the stony hills.
It folds abruptly and sinks to earth,
vanishing into sparse dry grass
like water into sand.

Enamelled gold and green,
the slender bodies fill an emu bush
with constant chatter
and slip through the thin, heat-toughened leaves
searching for seeds.

At the waterhole
scores drink at the edge,
footprints patterning the mud,
gold foreheads dipping,
gold throats lifting,
till at some hidden signal
they fly up in unison, a high coil of wings
and small parrot voices
fading into the arid distance.

Their cousins, in designer colours,
are shut in cluttered houses round the world.

Cadelga Outstation

In the night
all the corellas clapped up from the trees
over the waterhole.
On a shimmer of ghostly wings
they circled, screeching
like ploughshares in limestone.

A gypsy coin slid across the hollow palm
of heaven,
a breeze stirred the coolibahs, and
mouse-footed moon shadows
skittered over the earth.

Between the fallen stones of the ruined walls
roos lifted nervous heads
from the cropped grass.

Muted and muttering, corellas
settled back
to their branches. And an angel-
white feather
fell from the stars. Rocked
on air, floating
and sinking like a pearl shell swinging
through clear water,
it drifted
to the leaf-littered ground.

Tawny Frogmouth

Pinned by our torchlight
against night's pit-black curtain
the tawny frogmouth grips the powerline,
stretches his body upward,
and points his broad bill at Saturn,
reshaping himself
from bird
to broken branch.

No angled boughs
complete this deception
the smooth unbroken dark
betrays him. He stays
a moth-grey crotchet
printed on the stave of wires.

We douse the light. Let night
flow back for podargus.
Let him believe he has fooled us.

The Headland

Clouds are burning up into morning,
incandescent, swirling gold
and a feathering of silver
low to the ridge across the channel.

A pelican, steady on strong wings,
flies past the headland. Unalarmed,
great bill folded on her breast like a cutwater,
she keeps her course close by me.
Our glances meet
and hold.

On the brink of understanding
the calm behind that deep dark eye
I see her pass, watch her go
stroking slow wing-beats over the gilded water
into a sky by Turner.

With a sense of loss, of chances missed,
I turn away
and count five oyster catchers
prodding the beach for sea snails
below the point.

Mirror

the mirror's image
deceives
appears transparent but
is not
a blackness there
behind the silver gloss
deeper
than the bright fish-
star glinting
in wet reflections

I see and don't
see clearly
objects shown
are not tangibly there

a stage without
sound
where players mime and
gesture but
cut the thunder of Hamlet

a deafness trapped
behind glass
Poets Keep Out

MAIDEN VOYAGE
by **Ray R. Tyndale**

Ray Tyndale came to South Australia from England in 1970.
Past lives have seen her run a farm, bring up a family, direct an
acappella group, and work variously as cook, brickie, truckie,
economist, accountant, gardener, psychologist and even as a
Tupperware saleswoman. All of this rich life experience, and
more, informs her poetry. Lately, Ray has begun an exploration
of the Australian outback, not only enjoying hilarious and
intrepid adventures, but also looking more carefully into the
role of women in the bush today.

ACKNOWLEDGEMENTS

The Weekend Australian Review, Iron Lace, Sleeping Under a Grand Piano (ed. Geoff Page, Ginninndera Press: Canberra, 1999), Radio 5UV (Writers' Radio and State of the Arts), *Feast.*

For Peggy.

THE POEMS

I seduced her over dinner

She came laughing.
I watched
as she nibbled
brown bread croutons
with pheasant paté by
Maggie Beer and I murmured
as she played with
fettucine with cream and bacon
and lightly tossed green prawns.

I grilled for her
split black Genoa figs sprinkled
with demerara, garnished with
cool creamy marscapone.
We were neither of us young.
I toasted her eyes
with Cockatoo Ridge champagne
and we drowned in our desire.

ii   I moved into her life

I stayed
one night too long
and the family
wanted to see my credentials:
was I taking advantage
would I inflict another wound.

Like naughty children caught
with our fingers in the cake mix
we almost
                begged permission
from our juniors, then
laughing, flouted all the rules.

iii   I cooked up a storm

I sang to her, she played
for me straight from the music:
Brahms, Schumann, a prim
little piece of Bach. I sang
a quirky French love song and we
sat on the rug grappling
with Proust untranslated until,
growing bored with temps perdus

I cooked up a storm
in the kitchen and we picnicked
beneath the spreading elm trees
on baguettes stuffed à la Provençale
and a tarte of thinly sliced apple
dribbled with apricot jam and yellow cream
from Jersey cows grazing
rich Kangaroo Island pastures.
We became more compatible
with every shared meal.

iv Is this safe sex?

As I licked away
the sweet ripe mango
with its salty sauce
and as she spread Hudson's
Chocolate Rock icecream as
an encore there were no
anxious moments.

Maybe we should have considered
disease or violence or
incompatibility or outraged
daughters-in-law. Maybe
we should have had latex
instead of trust. Would such
considerations have affected
our consuming passion?

v One hundred years of cooking experience

I had cooked for years
and so had she but
never before had so much love
been ladled into the bouillabaisse, so
much care into the fegato
alla Veneziana, so much
attention to detail in such
ordinary things as mash and
cauliflower cheese and rice pudding.

Feeding the five thousand had been
a matter of habit
        unfed by desire.

vi A pigeon pair

I was the answer
to her mid-life crisis
and she to mine. The ex's
would find someone younger
to dish up the same old meals
on someone else's
wedding present dinner
service while she and I
could marry our talents
in the culinary department
with the coriander and the basil
and the raspberry coulis.

No need for unkeepable promises
as we peeled back the artichokes
sucking the lemon and butter from
fleshy leaves with our teeth
Wrapping our tongues around the
dripping hearts, little
moans of pleasure.
We had unfettered licence
to live and love and eat.

vii The New Cookbook for Longevity

After menopause a litany
begins of cholesterol and
blood pressure and rotting teeth
of gout and lumbago
and oesophagal spasm. I am
prey to all of these and so is she.
We lie and comfort one another
and plot the breaking of new rules.

Saltless vegetables with cumin, with
ginger or many cloves of garlic.
Caffeineless drinks with verbena
and geranium and sweet lemon balm.
Sugarless cakes with almonds, dates
and orange rind, dusted with cinnamon.
Olive oil instead of butter
sheeps milk yogurt instead of cream
ricotta instead of brie.
A wine-bottling with friends fills
the cellar with ruby-rich blood to be sipped
not sucked, drop by precious drop.

The feast goes on forever.

viii Finger food for frailty

She seduces me now
with Caesar Salad. Into my
mouth she dribbles the
lemon-soused croutons amid
anchovy-laden crisp cos lettuce.
She wipes her fingers sensuously
up my chin and I drool for her.
We share the crumbs of
soy and linseed bread scraped around
the bowl, last special morsels.

Such lucky women, she murmurs
as I tease her
with lemon sago pudding. She
wraps her tongue about the spoon.
We pour on more and more
thick coconut milk.
Old desire curls and flames.

I gave my love a plum…

Had Eve,
         rather than the apple
proffered in its place
a Narrabeen plum,
round and rosy
with soft yellow flesh,
dribbling juice with
each forbidden mouthful,
would the Knowing
of Original Sin have
offered more pleasure?

Falling together
among the sweet grasses
beneath the Tree,
licking
the sunburst residue,
nectar shared:
discovering there
that Knowledge can tender
         such bliss.

Maud

scant apologies to Tennyson!

Come my poppy
Fling open your flaming petals
Give to me your black heart.

Come my pansy
Toss back your knowing head
Share with me your secret thoughts.

Come my rose
Fill the air with your pungency
I will swim in your scented sea.

Come into the garden
My poppy, my pansy, my darling rose
Entwine with me.

The sun shall succour your black heart
The moon will keep your secret thoughts
And I will drown.

ii witch naked

She came in the garden.
The short summer grass
Tickled her brown bare feet.

And that not all:
She played hide-and-seek
Through the Queen Anne's lace.

Flinging here a shirt
There a belt to dangle
Like stars upon the frangipani.

Witch naked, she dived
Head first into the herbaceous border
Made a nest beneath the dahlias.

The shards of sunlight spun spells
The bumble bee sucked nectar
And oh! my poppy, my pansy, my rose,
            There sucked I.

iii spellbound in the garden

Witch naked
She flaunted through the walled garden
The empty park solstice-lit.

She twitched
The fallen leaves with her brown toe
The moonlight rippled and sparked.

She put a pointed finger
Into the throat of a foxglove
It lifted its head to her.

She picked a poppy, a pansy, a rose
Pricked her finger on a thorn
Bled upon the camomile, the baby's tears, my heart.

I swept the path
With her broomstick.
Together we rode the moonbeams.

iv together in the garden with love

Knowing you're there
Working alongside
In the garden
Heightens the pleasure,
Eases the load.

You do the weeding
     I mow the lawns.
You wield the shears
     I fill the bin.
The poppy, the pansy, the rose
Flourish with your care.
We suck the blood from each other's
Fingers, stabbed to the heart
By rose thorns.

I pick the salads for dinner
You cut the flowers for the house.
Together in the garden
We weave our own witchery.

Click

Arkaroola, The Gammon Ranges, SA

From the ridge top
The tourist
Skims the surface of the world:
Beaut skies, great colours,
Amazing views-
Hey darl, hold it right there!

Over there in the view
Ten thousand roos a year
Are shot without denting the numbers.

Over there in the view
The soil blows away
By the tonne every day.

Out on the plain,
Dry creekbeds wind redgums
Into white Lake Frome where,
No sweat,
You can walk on water.

Look through the shutter
See one cow per thousand acres
Flyblown fat-tailed wild sheep
Herds of stocky goats
See the multinational pastoralist
The ever hopeful prospector
The last elder of the Adnyamathanha –

Hey darl, smile!

Farina Ruins

In SA's Far North

It's not the bitter wind
rolling unhindered across the stony plain,
miles of nothing
as far as the eye can see;
It's not the wind
that makes my eyes water / at Farina.

The only tree
grows through the Post Office roof.
The only grass grows, unnibbled
inside the railings of unmarked graves.
The only sign of life
the detritus of human living.

> a midden of broken bottles
> a rusted kerosene 'fridge
> a collapsed cellar
> an underground bakery oven
> > that will never again
> > fill the town
> > with homely smells

Hardship with nothing to show.
A railhead to push to the pastures
which must be greener
over the hill.

Afghans brought lifeblood unthanked,
Aborigines worked for no pay,
rainclouds dispersed into dust,
    babies died
        hopes extinguished.

Farina, 'Granary of the North',
it's not the wind
that makes my eyes water.

Barra' Tart

The truckies' favoured pitstop
between the Alice and the Top End

is a rough little place
in Barrow Creek.

Just some pumps and a rutted
forecourt and a dunny

down the back, but old Ma Fisher
as they all call her

not only makes the best burgers
in the Territory but also

a treacle tart,
best any sheila ever cooked.

They screw up their sweat-smeared faces
and shout

"Come on you old fart, give us
some more tart!"   It's got

the colour and smell of hot bitumen.

Farmer's wife

The cows milked and the chooks shut up
The bread baked and the dishes done
The pickers' pay packeted and the books up-to-date
The garden watered and fresh flowers in the house
Homework supervised and a square meal eaten
The tractor spares ordered and the vet assisted
at a post-mortem
on a hand-reared calf
a yearling
that's now a dead loss.

No need for Serapax or Mogadon or Valium
No need for Horlicks or Milo or hot milk
The farmer's wife sleeps every night
the sleep of total exhaustion
She groans with relief
as her body unfolds
onto the mattress and
as he clambers on top of her
like the prize Poll Hereford bull
in the paddock
she is beyond caring.

She is rocked to sleep already thinking
of what tomorrow brings when the pickers arrive
at five.

Burial

The dead calf slithers,
Flayed bone and scabby skin,
Off its bier and into the scarred darkness
    Of the disused well.

She covers the corpse
With shovelsful of dirt.
Hand into the small of her back,
    She sighs at the waste.

In the leaden afternoon,
She buries the sorrows
Of the drought-stricken land,
    While the eucalypts droop.

Clapping the dirt from her hands
She gets on with the work of the day:
Battling the scourge of
    Unbalanced books.

the blooding

Appraising the virgin copy of a poem
is a thrust to the heart
of the poet's ego.

Neither a rape nor a courting,
whatever is said or left unsaid
probes like a speculum.

Is it innocence or pride
that is deflowered
by critical analysis?

However studied the response
the whole being protests
the misunderstanding, the insult.

Words may be changed, modified
upon reflection, but reluctantly,
without modesty.

The taker of maidenhead
is the first reader, the audience
for whom the poem is written.

maiden voyage

i... in utero

How did they make me?
In the middle of war
Flying bombs whistling
Blackout, rationing, ack-ack guns.

In an air raid, a coupling
Risked out of the shelter?
In a field of autumn wheat,
Dog-fight overhead?
In a moment of passion or
With a sharp cry of fear?

Conceived in war
Undernourished in the womb
Vomited into a world fighting itself
How did they make me
Fleshed and strong-boned
Unruffled and determined
At all costs
To avoid conflict?

ii… maiden voyage

I remember nothing
Of my birth.
Three days of useless pushing
No room for me to emerge:
Cut like a Roman emperor
But a girl, another girl
And not the Ides of March.

I remember nothing
Of infancy.
Of suckling and swathing,
The world coming into focus.
The comforting touch
The anxious caress
The timid gentle song:
Nothing.

Photographs
Black and white, edge-torn
Reminder on the back
In fountain pen
My mother's hand:
        My christening
        A pram in the snow
        The nurse with white cap
        A beaming cousin
        Ringleted big sister, solemn
        A bare embarrassment on
                a handmade bunny rug.

I existed. I am there
In the faded photos,
Admired and posed
Staring into the lens.
I remember nothing.
My lifeline had started
As if without me.

iii... climbing stairs

Two years into peacetime
I was two also.
My sister was at school
I had my mother to myself
Yet she is not there
In my dreams, my recollections.

Was I a self-centred child
That I needed no companion?
Wrapped in my own world
Of house and stairs,
Garden and cot

I could reach out a finger
Touch the droplet of water
At eye-level, in the pink cupped
Petals of the windflower.

I could climb three stairs
To the landing, turn around,
Slip down again slowly
On my rump, one two three
Bump bump bump
And do it again.

I could tease apart
The red-painted babushka
Find the baby inside
The mother inside the
Grandmother. Put them back
Together and knock them over
To bob up again
On their rounded bottom.

Learning to touch
To feel   to listen
To see   to be endlessly
Curious; to be me.

iv… weaned

Still in a pram at three
But denied the breast,
Bread and milk sops
Gave me rosy cheeks
In bitter winter.

To have been breast fed
For so long and to remember
Not one suck   one fondle
One drop of warm sustenance
Is such deprivation.

I am left
With a loathing
For boiled milk.

Foundations I

When her corsets no longer held
Her public persona rigid and proper,
Mother sent for the corsetiere.

A little girl, I watched the tape wound
Deftly around ample bosom fully clad –
Courteous measurement, modesty sustained.

They murmured together as my mother bent
And stretched, turned and stood, maintaining
Dignity over this garment of control.

"Double laced at the back for shape and
Hooks are easy down the front, new metal
Stays are longer lasting, rubber-stopped for comfort.

Bend forward, madam, for the cup size." Such
Intimacy in the touch, the voice, such tact.
A mutual understanding of social etiquette.

I wasn't welcome at the fitting.
No-one but Father saw her
Without her corsets;
Mother's tight figure
                    Upheld propriety.

Worksheds

Remembering Robert Botcherby Tindale (Roy) 1907-1972

Many childhood hours spent watching
at her father's elbow
in his shed
her face raised to his,
chattering:
she was a talkative child
watching as he worked
learning to be the son
he never had.

A modest shed,
just outside the kitchen door
not quite detached from the
womb of the house.
Tar paper roof
rough timber walls
unclad and cobwebby
masculine but warm,
a safe place to be.

Laid out on the wooden workbench
were the parts of a carburettor
an idle fobwatch
a partly-made picture frame
and the saw-eroded mitre box.
Resin-filled wood shavings
unpaired nuts and bolts
perished rubber grommets rolled
on the busy surface: *you never know,*
it might come in use.

He prided himself on his skill
at dismantling, with care and delicacy.
No-one was cruel enough
to ask that he mend or repair:
a man of great charm, his delight sufficed.

So the child stood at his side and she learnt
how engines work, how clocks work,
how electric plugs work
how to use a brace and bit
a coping saw, a jack plane
a spokeshave and a carborundum stone.
She learned to curl
the fingers of her left hand
beneath the sole of the plane
and watch the shavings crinkle
            and fall.

She learned to build special jigs
to bore an angled hole
to dovetail drawers
and hollow-bevel a chisel.
She was eager to please and
happy to learn. She was nearly
as good as a son.

Given away early in marriage
she watched in disbelief
her young husband's clumsy attempts
to change a plug
or use a new plane, a gift
from his father-in-law.
Had he not learnt
these things from his father?

Her carefully learned skills
were well-honed in marriage
but her sons could not learn
        from Mother.
They turned   their young faces
away in disgust and shouted *Mum!*
        It's not cool!

As the men
faded from her life
she dusted off her memories
and set up her own workshed.
A place of pleasure
learning new skills to complement
the old and practising them
on gifts for friends:
exquisitely turned boxes in
sandalwood, olive and home-grown
              nectarine
silky oak knife handles
soft, aromatic salad bowls
of bird's eye huon.
Remembering
the father's delight.

Her life is dismantled now
but not left undone
like Father's fob watch.

The passing of time has
set her free
and in the fastness of
her own shed
she can share her father's delight.

Friendly Street Reader 24

EDITED BY RAY STUART AND JUDE AQUILINA

The Friendly Street Rocket blasted off from Gordon
Choon's old fireworks factory in 1975, careered through
the Cosmos for over 20 years, and now cruises into the
Millennium – its crew the best of the South Australian
poets who read at the Box Factory in 1999.

ISBN 1 86254 508 1

WAKEFIELD PRESS

Knifing the Ice

JUDE AQUILINA

Jude Aquilina writes in a fresh contemporary voice, with insight and humour. Whether she takes you to the fridge, the bathroom or the moon, you will see vivid new horizons. Espy the clandestine life of warts; taste the warm bite of a full-chested cheese; fraternise with flashers and fungi.

Experimental in ideas and form, Jude's poetry is sensuous and surprising. Some poems shine 'like a jewel in an idol's forehead', while others should be wrapped in brown paper!

Jude's poetry is refreshingly accessible… the reader easily identifies with the images and hears the rhythm of the lyrics.
Martin R. Johnson

… the sudden effective image, the mundane made magical'.
Steve Evans

ISBN 1 86254 509 X

WAKEFIELD PRESS

Friendly Street New Poets One

GEOFF KEMP, YVE LOUIS, JOHN MALONE

ISBN 1 86254 346 1

Friendly Street New Poets Two

ANNA BROOKS, JENNY WEIGHT, DAVID COOKSON

ISBN 1 86254 374 7

Friendly Street New Poets Three

LOUISE NICHOLS, STEPHEN LAWRENCE, RICHARD HILLMAN

ISBN 1 86254 405 0

Friendly Street New Poets Four

JUNICE DIREEN, JULES LEIGH KOCH, JASON SWEENY

ISBN 1 86254 446 8

Friendly Street New Poets Five

IOANA PETRESCU, MAUREEN VALE, JULIAN A. ZYTNIK

ISBN 1 86254 447 6

WAKEFIELD PRESS